SHIT TO SHUTTLE

NAGMAA JAINEEKART CHAUHAN

Made with ♥ on the Notion Press Platform
www.notionpress.com

to my muma

to her marred dreams

to my flows and blows

Contents

Preface

seeking , solitude, solemnly

Acknowledgements

Prologue

I encompass diversity of the places, people, culture in me .Started writing with silence inside and out at the age of ten to god about my class marks and some teachers like shark .But found it so sound in writing In school poetry was seen as work of perverts and not tempted much .in my teenage found no space out of my solitude where i could confine . But chunk of poems I wrote covertly now build my confidence . As only my diary has witnessed my shifting stories and theories. I accept the fact that there is lot of space for refinement but I assure it'll be worth reading . After a long day of toil and your mind on boil .I don't think anyone would be interested in reading something factual and heated turmoil .It should be something dulcet memories renewing regaining and this book does this magic

Life ; not a fairy garden that allows cherry picking all unseasonal fruits in tabled manner .It's wilderness where you will bump into thorns and at times into thrones ; same does my book .

Bonn appetite poetry smackers!!

I'm grateful to all woes and joys infused on my ways which made me jot down my parents , the trees, nature ,creatures, my surrounding palace, my cherished upbringing,all inspiring forces holding me .

*out of thickets to tickets *

reminisce

Faded memory of five

Is that of the litchi tree in Mussoorie ; I peeped out in my striped frock from that large window.Is that of my mumma washing my face in thecold water stream flowing downhill from upper reaches.Is that of the glistening night of Dehra. Of that clear water of pool which lured me with its shining pebbles down .I dipped and drowned nearly ; got asylum in my father's water tube somehow after fluttering my wings .Is that of red robe monks in row on far distant hills .Me climbing up posing for pictures .

winters

Gleamed with scene of beauties and I'm one of them Liberation is something I'm into .Entering joy exempted of all the taxes have to pay for feast in.

Twilight

A cart passes

jingling anklets horse

Dancing on road pores

I wrong for new bride on floor

Monsoon

It's raining out calming my inner storm of hundred nights.

With the onset of monsoon

I let my tears fell on floor Which were in eyes for long

To flow with the raindrops on shore To meet the confluence

Where we swore not to be the clone for another cyclone

*

I'll neglect the storm lately

But the naked umbrella and

Dislocated roof won't let me

trust the stillness of wind again

-they are saying nothing has changed

*

"you must be living in high towers

boasting it all hours

terrace farms and grants

but the smell of earth is here on ground only"

3 a.m.

I got up found Orion patrolling the sky as some hunter on fight and pole star on punctual rent stretching the sky to north as main rope of closing night tent ."there is grave mountain ahead of grief eye savouring of hills and rills on screen but far away from screams"

4 a.m.

I pluck an four O'clock and ask it for time it showed 'BLOSSOM'.

A morning affirmation"""" *Grievances are grave but you' re brave*

5 a.m.

In dawn coolness star shivers and sky put off the shimmering gown and drapes a white blanket .

dawn sky drove away

Intertwined with all existing shades

Without discriminate dark, light, deep shallow ,dull and lull

Ready to merge into without marking verge

All ready to embrace new phase

From stormy to shiny , frill to still ,vivid to void

It's we only Who discriminate colours to debates

razing away races with blades

colliding complexions often with perfections

Sprinkle happiness serum on your sinister thoughts -most effective beauty serum

6 a.m.

I had my thoughts in tow and I moved out to see the unpaid live show of peacock squawk, sprinting clouds birds chorus singing , hide and seek of twigs after leaves . I spot butterfly fluttering A common grass yellowI take butterfly poseFeel levitating in morning -*Yoga*

7:30 a.m.

I see jungle babbler withit's orchestra drawing near to me after I've started spending early hours sitting out I guess we're friends from now "*these are strong winds which open and closes the doors slow winds doesn't cave in any ray"don't be afraid of gusty winds*

honey loops

LIFE was best until loops had no

meaning other than honey loops to me .

6: 15 p.m. august

Oggy with it's mother Lucy chasing the monkey away without bark silently to curb noise pollution . breezy evening .Oggy had become stray but now wants me to keep holding its hands after someone bited it out

The little boy resembles you

Hails from your native state

Appears before as small rabbit from bush

Has a wide grin Gluing my sights to his Small eyes

Has a charm drawn from your canvas

rise at Rishikesh

From chaotic cunning surrounding of Delhi ,a morning we started by evening was amid *Ganga Ghats* . I was in grim sheer dilemma having words with my inner seer .It was bright evening with cool zephyr all draining their thoughts and boats in the waters .Trolling around glinting souvenir markets , those sequence lights were tempting than any hungry city lights .I was exhausted after long walk on periods .After we were done with jumping on the bed .a miracle happened as I checked my laptop ; my eyes were smeared with smiling.I slept draping on my tearful eyes bulged out from past days downslide . Secretly awoke early morning for rejuvenating walk after days of juvenile jitter As god lock doors for long before silver lining the same that morning door keys were with sleepy hotel staff Swift winds and bell sounds were enveloped round the hills walked towards *ghat*after I was pulled off my main mast through narrow turning street lanes an open space ;smoothning the sharp rocks with its pious waters I bowed called *maiya !!ganga maiya !!*. I was sentimental Out of an exodus it was all empty to fill all new I wished .Did yoga with my muma and she denied to go down near the swift waters I obeyed .

Sauntering down on streets I bought morning treats . I ducked into a small broken glass window to stand on the road facing hill tops and balconies Had bath and was ready to flow again after blow .While breakfast the serving elderly man was so amiable that those generous *pahadi gens* couldn't be overlooked.I was restored and moved away from the place before my thoughts moved along with the saffron robes .Took road to *Dehra* veering away from *Tehri* . I was trespasser from plains surrendered there collating I was no less than in broad fraud. ' the face of defeat is ugliest '

11 p.m. Asked my body for the ransom to release my soul It replied – life .Said don't reel under feel under me. Don't run away from me .On road to mussorrie the views were sight for my sore eyes.The longing was to brake the car and to write beside a stream ; a persisting longing . Dipped my feet in small stream for half hour in quite crowded tourist spot. "I'm jet lagged on those lofty mountain passes where there're no heart passes . "

29 august 1:30 PM In between mountains

And my heart sank deeper Down in origin

of those earthly thermal fountains for warmth

which was absent in every manly arms

landslides of emotions ,erosion of every atomic question

those boulders fallen created hollow

portions can't be filled by those potions

Tehri! Ohh tehri!

Old tehri!!I complain

thy people drown other's in city

You were like ;that old lost city

Which fewer had seen But those who had seen

Were Flooded with devotion

Your charm was vulnerable as like that of submerging

splendid king's palace on highland

carried my censorious eye camera before the view vanish

ran through corridors

like a flamingo or some tropical bird after mango

High walls of dam capped fury of those living above waters

I capped in gaps your last memories to

prevent the future smash from rising feelings as bash

that could create all trash in one flash

The outburst of dam gates drowned the whole city

My whiskly outburst could drown you infinity

Obviously new city is based on beauty

But the old clock tower

drowned feel guilt for its building

advisor whose tick-tick is still heard

only by olds fearing gods

who could stop the *sangam* ahead

of those two rivers

flowing since there were no viewers

the dam? Or those who put the rocks and rights against dynamite ?

or the striking embark of thoseriver rafts

gliding over the lengths of river belittling it as dwarf

none !no one could !

each year with its revocable revenges

and unmoored mind

sweeping roofs leaving no proofs ,

mushrooming over stays and false prays

it deflect of its path to desolate your enigmatic engineer math

January

Burning midnight oil not literary but actually as electricity has gone .Sky is thundering disturbed with western disturbances might get burst into tears as downpour soon

February

Love in air .try to not to fall in snare. Put on face mask its dare . It's all lush green in the surrounding except my heartwhich is deserted -drought

*if sunsets and sunrise are not fighting for their

incomparable beauty and duty then why you and me *? honey!*

*

March mornings

Some are iridescent

Some are etched with indelible ink of mutual understanding

Those little steps over trails were short in distance

But thoughts were spinning from swearing to new bearing

If I ever become mum or numb

Then don't shun

En route to your journey you may find many churny

But believe most are cheesy

Don't doubt my ecstasy I'm bit messy

April 17 6.am -on vacations of afflictions

Breach of bliss

Auction of feelings on the land of heart

with swords of words maimed the soul

now will resurrect only in next birth

I slept with thoughts knocking and begging me straight way .I took pity and they unhealed wickedly .My eyes are tired with last night blubber .But now lively as if the rising sap . facing the sun now. I looked at those green dwellers ;where these residents does not dwell I never feel settled there .

Yards -The back' the front' the side one

I see u ,I'm used to see u

That in your absence

I got caught in flue -green emerald

May

May we meet again ! Natural meets are unmatched flowers are ointments on crooked hearts.

mela

A night with music heights

another with crying sights *-the fair dispersed taking away all my all fairness of my heart*

June

I tookPause! Looked back on dairy pages full of chorus silently sitting at one of the busiest junctions found what I'm doing is my desired function that I forgot facile for further promotions.

July

My body clock went against the world clock and I switched off my phone; the major cacophony and found I've still few hours left .

The lost firefly in me

is the long left 'line' she could not follow

telling herself as part of 'circle'

which then unveiled as a spiral 'loop' of plight

snatching 'square ' meals at night

and trapping the free noise of vowel to mere passing towels *-I'm unfullfiled dream of her*

Aug 5 p.m.

I planted purslanes .far delicate like roses and grow where it find suitable like moss away from polluted boss.that's how got its name ' rose moss . '

Autumn when I touched my rock bottom

Oh thy leaves falling

My heart is peeling off its healings

Calling for another zealings

Heyy! Uhh dealing with those feelings

Trust me you're in my longings

willl be in your bondings while howlings

but you've only cold scoldings - *Undermining my thoughts you re finding faults*

Autumn equinox

Knock !knock !Hii summer

Autumn with its beloved winter knocked on my door

With last memories of late summer

Asked if you're there with me

And I burst

Seasons passed!

Imprisoned turned dark !

Mortal passed!!

I passed half!!

With no mark ofyour shaft or raft

Festivals passed!! With creating only cavities

I brought down all the lamps and ladders changed our analogous colours

to some neutral dweller and expedited for a long evening walk out

without left doubts ,slamming the door on the face of seasons

locking them in my bygone division changing my vision with

reason that everthing was foolish fusion of my oblivion

September evening

I do cat walk on muddy trails of their garden .crush mango leaves to smell the June freshness. Sighed ripping mandarins .help myself with two large green grapefruits At noon walking over sun burnt soil Bricks wrapping heat like a foil.

**Clouds be like* passing souls *

Which don't sustain for long

At times burst upon in a grey groan

At times dust on frivolous white foam

At places perspire While at places persist as desire

At hours knit the sky like unsifted wires

At hours sift away like withering flowers

At minutes displace from a space

At minutes throng a place

October

Sickness sustains .hello medicines! Thanks for keeping me in your accounts .typhoid in tears, lack of gears.no one in wish list .I went to doctor for my ailment suggested a regime without finding if it was ruling inside .

'I shall wait for thy

To exchange look again on bonfi'e -bonfide'

November

I long to sit out in the evening

While dreaming us two

live streaming in garden

meandering ,murmuring ,navigating

throughhurdlings catching up goals

like tossed up ball in the court

december

An early winter twilight where our sights met for that short flight

I made mayday calls

Which were undetected

by your radio waves

- Commercial pilot Out of plane in bus lane

*

They called me selfish

For using their emptiness to fulfillg myself

-don t care about north ,south and their mouth

*

Tinderbox exploded!!!

The most surprising present I've ever unboxed is the school tiffin .After a hard work out –teachers scolds, paper folds , Desk duels with some mind mules .

The bell rings! all rush out of flinch forgetting the autocratic reigning regime. The secret box is opened slyly and tinderbox explode in the class when *rice* with *rajma* in tiffin ready to embrace .you're the boss then .biggest blessing .tiffin make your day and you offer the pray for the longevity of the rice rajma couple . Start gulping down as poison so that other don't show interest in the couple's chemistry which is scrumptiously good .The maths teacher who has survived in the havoc , strong storm ,heavy rain and brain drain, forgets the counting and count on his colleagues chappatis drains all their quantity to null and their mind void ,who later thought of deploying him out of this geoid .

the geography teacher lost his access to his own axis circles freely in orbit like our ISRO's economical but efficient satellite reaching the destiny after revolving for long same does this man involving , revovlving round the best packet While, the polity teacher wasn't done with policy making how to eat his tiffin whether to be liberal or to act according to cerebral a single sniff let him decide to make it his exclusive right to eat every bite. While mister harry and Charlie, the language teacher were busy eating today's writer in their brunch baking a new verse out of their thesaurus trust . I with my

balanced diet munching slowly while others were done minutes before
making salad burgers stuffed with facts for next lecture's test.

*

Surreal week days

Soonday - passes thinking for the next day's match with surprise workpacks

.

Moan day- why you arrive I've met another deadline

Twodays – ohh !take your prize today successfully passed a day

Wining day – half battle won

Thrust day – strategy for weekendis planned on this day

Freak day - the dead worm turn to butterfly but in stomach

Super day - Saturday! Saturday !

*

From rivalries to rosaries

That year !That last year! Mere year

Those who never spoke they came alive

After years of sleep

Not willing in school

has turned to living in school

those jails years has turned into bail years

last year no uttering has turned into buttering

this twelve has a spell

even escape but wanna recap

*

Finding pair of sock out of mountain of washed clothes

On school mornings is unfeasible than digging treasure out of earth

*

those arched ways where i wrote my own horoscope

Notions are not your nations

They said.... notions are not your nations

I wondered why ? but those swathes are sweet

but showed me those freeways with bright stars

guided not to be the lamp for stars

there'll be supernova

I wondered why Brought me down on those freeways with bright stars

Found these ways wide as wounds

So guideeeee .....I mmmm side

Buh'd bide as bride

Said words 'll come along with u

Those same identical ways where

life flung them to present

Became anonymous

star became anonymous finding galaxy

became a clarity that it'll met its obituary in early years of century

Come my way there'll be stitches

'll keel down in ditches

You 've to fix my glitches

Said 'put paid to those ditches

Are not your niches

-to my teacher

*

Turned the back for the best

but for the chest it was halt

left the sights which were holding my kites

those doors became dormant

hard those height that left without hope

God call for my bail

I'm no longer in this sail"

- dead more than alive

*

monsoon in south

It was first when I saw a giant snake in real that rattles on rails outside of zoo . I boarded cum jammed in with my belongings without beacon of hope of ever unboarding .the illusion cum fear of coming down from upper berth resulted in gluing to window seat with unprecedented scenes and squeal of train wheels that kept me awake , sometimes swarming over insects gossips anight stops while sometimes vendor's snacks .

Motors for morbid moots, tongas for touch with roots and I was rooted in early morning hours .moist coal aroma air in kopargaon as we boarded off . At stay I was doodling with unnatural colours on phone screen in my daddy's phone was amazed to undo redo colours leaving no residues and who knew I will miss the natural colours which will blur or fade but will not vanish fully

A yellow leaping frog on muddy roads posing for photos while plodding .damp wet western Ghats of Nashik from that minibus . Of wooden boat rowing against stream of *Godavari.* Of those hundreds untouched water falls of woods. that big wild rat that slammed my sulky mood of spending the rest on streets.

.For many days the skyline of the place I compared with silhouette of trees and clouds far to feel quite respite from my mountain sprite .It was here I first made cone of my hand ate meals without spoon and later remained half starved whenever tried eating with spoon .

before life set a satire

Sunset dates are fixed my mate

wolf out and taste every zest take

eye off the blunder move out for another wonder

With every single blow you will get extra glow

Lay off laxity and grab serenity in perplexity

halk out your another move out

work for it all day in and day out

look out through window chink

your life would be filled with several inks

With dopamine dice Throw on cloud nine

"Bed time affirmation-

Descended here not simply for demise"

I look up to thsese friends of mine

amla

Pine in plains

From my window

Shows greet

Its branches swings down

Very inviting

Bees a bride

Garlanding it

Bowing down

You'refruitless despite your full grown size. you've seen me crying sleepin gawake, laughing from that window consoled me with your shade

Sweet lime

You are bitter and tasteless but I have known you from puberty we both embraced it together .

Peach

We have known each other from few years .the fence kept us aloof .you are beautiful. I have to await to see u flowering for long .They fell for your beauty and toppled you down their definition of love 'falling and then felling .'

Grapefruit

I keep eyes on fruits for long .but give away to relatives when you ripe . I think we should reconcile over this unfair treaty

Guava

You are great staying friend you have taught me hunting gathering huh!.As while plucking I need to toil and your green fruits play hide seek camouflage against your pale green leaves You have acted as all situation friend. Serving me with twigs for my teeth and fruits for my savour .

North Indian rosewood

We were neighbours for long .but started noticing in recent years only. Your canopy is deep. Make my thought pensive for a brief .

Java plum

I take you for granted and when you shed your all fruits . I repent for not being close to you enough to miss you daily.

Mango

Thanks for your freshness that fascinated me to eat despite the fact I'm not mango lover. Your fresh leaves brings in freshness.

Weeping fig

Auncle !You're pole straight . You've seen me since I was a kid. You act as defensive wall and has stolen several badminton shuttle and playing balls .auncle I've never broken your leafy windows . when will you return all those balls .

The simple friend

On festivals days with my tiny hands not reaching up to windowsill . I used to carry hangings of lined white paper secretly torn from my notebooks and few from coloured scrap books ; the best décor. the cleaning cum winnowing dust over the room was so effortful .Those heavy wooden carved doors I see nowhere now.

It's about a place where time does not flies like mountains my grannie house where it was sole silent like midnight past 8 in the bustling city , where I had exclusive right over the snacks . where my fake news reported from the incorrectly spelled only places I had known then had one audience .

Her stories of sarus cranes , sparrows ,deer's ,mynahs can't be sourced from *wiki* .I used to be super famished of her stories at supper times coiling in heavy quilts of natural sun dry fumes

Story time ended! Now I'm writing stories .

Asked for a gift and I presented something which will surpass centuries -

piece of my writing

Ablated apart from my diary

Throbbing part of my body

Donated to your wealth

that space remains void

until I don't avoid

no attached page ever can

replace that one torn page

which enlightened my days

like a sage or paid wage

for years of my sustain in cage

*

they said '*what word mean forget !word bears no essence*

Words in my words

when my tongue fell

with a thud on my mouth floor

trapped in by those standing out-doors

when lost all taste bud

then words shaped taste

word kept alive with enticing traits

word ushered in light

harbouring both pride and hide

words are meant to be kept

while speech is for spit out without drawing draft

words are meant to craft cutting with sharp wedges

all shrewd edges words mere words put thumbprints

on my windpipe pressing my throat to rotten dead life note

Love today is swapof body maps

-Get up from the false nap ,

each person wish to read

map of all beautiful cities

Were You aware your eyes would harm my soul you looked agog at ?

They rightly said 'it's the places that decide your virtue ; out of your beautiful place

you met in wrong place of deceit

Boarded a train

from*Kalka to Shimla* with my toy heart

convivial in that toy train

I was stupefied for those sec while I was emptied of all my colour sets

clear rills were of your colour

brooks were so bending as if my tongue babbling

tracks were jagged as if your teeth lent for flex

white of snow was glinting as if had your glimpse

while bear lurking from leaves

to make a fable out of what we talked in that cable

that dangling cliff to mountain recalled

me of your smile with what my heart was clinging

those descending down clouds towards sloppy slides

restoredthe longing to touch your dear feet down

far flung hues on hills of buttercups

evoke us two draped in golden husk

when we saw us first

as if deer got its lost musk

on reaching altitudes a rosy tint

climbed upon my cheeksas if you draped on your

strawberry sweater on a pale creek

the sour green apple I ate

restirred the greenery wrapped round you

the cracks in rock protrude after rain

reminded how your cracked

heel cudgelled my brain

I was reading supplementary

found we're complementary

and book fell out of my hand

train terminated Shimla

!Shimla!Shimla !

reminded how we met between book

s and remained only in my books

as like that fire erupted in jungle

remain confine to forest only

never reaches and harm another out

all what I recall is highly endemic to me only

while you were like that migratory bird

which abandon places

with each squeak in search

of a new fruit for its sharp beak

Meeting you was as dark as that tunnel that takes to funeral

I'm turning tovoid without

you and fuller at the same

Your writings are so tragic

That I effort to write mine

with invisible vivid inks

Which leave behind no imprints

Those sufferings are so skulling

That I deny myself as a person

of bones but of stones

With empty stomach

I miss you

With full I kiss u

I doesn't trust other lips

Which dip me in clicks of hips

But yours bring me out

of all those false fix

-mumma

I see her changing sides

All night

Checking the strain mark in Fear

And tires to hide it

As if negative remark

Which none wish to be marked

So before one sees

Ties her white scarf

Which get paints in

red bleeding bark goes to wash off

in ignominious dark

at times when dreadful

spirits wander and get terrify

one vanishing the blood clot

one daubing the blood being a clot

-Insuperable handicap

*

Sleeping straight

On these dates is my fate

Becoming stewards At the age

when you're someone's ward

give rise to high tides

when you are simply boy of your time

and I become that time zone

Of one more life

-I am the architect behind lives

Two hands met is stairs

One had to move slightly up

One had to move slightly down

Without caring about the crown

Those looking for equity in love are clown

-leap together

The one who swells and dwells

On the sunlight is left

To confront those eye heartening lights

which left all blind in search of that client

who'll brighten their lives

through bribes while trapping them in

those cold concrete sites promising tall heights

resulting only in perpetual sui-cides

you fly high in skies with maiden flies

while I count my sliver locks

turning fright seeing those price

putting lock on those serving diets

in undelight tight life undecibled voices in times

of high ear tearing sound

of honks and pseudo social monks .

-I'm that radio tuned voice Which can nevfeel tuned on your new music tape fuelled by internal heat

hands ,hairs as my

tentacles strewed

on the bed which

on touching something stubbly

Composed like a

small fish seeing a shark

-touch of animal in guise of man

You are not gentle; someone added

Roses have spikes ,darling

boast beauty in each behold

too delicate get worn easily on hold

spikes are meant to jolt

those jerks touching like jelly

or vault for support

then throwing away once

satisfying their pseudo influx

smelled to coax

by many obnox using

its smell to hoax

- roses and porcupines are same

Was in ship, not in sea

Yet was bout to drown

Was in blaze

But shining like a glaze

So told that I'm in haze

Was in my ears, buh'd not in dears

Yet gave some cheers and hears

Was a humane, not insane

after some lame fame

So I told my inhumane ,was stark as bark,

buh'd got mark in my heart park

the ship terminated,

buh'd that gratefulness

in still boarding and moulding

-To the good spirits I came across

Unhook anchor rooted inmisbelief and

the dustypal from your ship i.e., on voyage to your dreamland.

Comes from

A stunning wasteland of beauty

extreme heat and imperial beat

extreme cold conspires fear in folds

-roots

*

Your hills must be the

place of youthful zing

But these echoes eyes

of those undaunt forces

fought on horses

-Aravallis

verses

In kitchen

With the sweat dripping under my knees

I laugh with cheesefor your appease

serve you even if I sneeze like storm breeze

heart kneading red with pale

renouncing all what I get for inhale

buying all the sooty in sale being a chimney veil

-middle class Indian working mother

pre-diwali cleansing

I Passed from his home

Which was lately an epitome of

‘ our home’

Found all what we had given to each other

incline , adrenaline , belongings ,longings

Were out in sun

we never belonged to this turn

or long run ; I felt

- short run

Spices

I touched you

And lost my all taste

Giving all to others

Realized you were only a mix-on

that I was trying to make-on my life

While you were part of *sickening food *

With what I was thinking of preparing a * salubrious mood *

The swirl of oil fume ;it was the stove removed all

I had for spices in my hand

*

Spilling right now out of hearts

now going in different directions

-Enchanting faces and flies

holi

Felt would be scot-free after self-flagellation

may be wrongly performed the ritual

The process:

-Airbrushed my wounds

-Like flowery grounds

- let others dance on those suppurating sore sounds

- never reproached until went out of restoration

Mirage has created

Into my eyes

That is why I turned so blind

Leaving all behind

Headed to find your signs

In Place dotted with only thorny pines and cactus wines

reached an already availed oasis

protests in my proses

are prosaic to your clauses

*

Not a train berth

You reserved once hooked on baggage

and left all once reaching your play station

Not excerpt in your life

I'm unread novel of affinity

-not for sojourn

I don't listen to songs

Because its not same as it's shown

After duels Bruises ,bulged eyes

Are missing in frames

Missing the chance to be in fame

I've cried for long

Now I want to smile

If u thrive Beside without

Being cyanide

Massive undercount

if I neglect

at dusk can see cattle grazing maize

Tinkle of bells in my mails

While rain Can see soaking grain

Farmer's grind of vein

brain surefing out of membrane in an open plain plane

fallen fence still separating

golden fall on leaves raising

profound loss if I don't found

petrichor snoring all fancy perfume fog

weeds sprouting out knowing soon will be uprooted out

thought of being broil does not let them kill their baby in embroil

smile in those slums ; stillness of splendour plums

They played a song called “ peace ”

And all geese dispersed away fan stops!

Spread of air

steps in stairs

birds preening in air and I hear ?

bushes telling themselves

that they care not anymore

to play music for earthly fair

and will soon enter a sphere without any heir

Globe as farming bed

People as produce of that bed

On every bed there is different crop and raindrop

different vegetable and label

different seed and weed

Each having different harvesting season

ripening season and different blooming vision

But down is all same

Without any ornamental petal and mesmerizing battle with bees

ringed by worms and different mud forms ,dread norms

rooted by god to stop mayhem

but in race of getting uprooted for name

brain

frail like a coriander seeded in summer rain

heart

Some steal

this one squeezed

me out of my fleece

being cold degree freeze

-replaced from kidney to appendix

while I was trying to enter the heart which that beats without care

legs

I wobble

While plod

As if flickering candle

Trying best to hold

While them as gusty winds

trying to blow me out creating a musty

suffocative environment shroud

-You were a Flamingo

Turned to vulture Later

*

If the ants are marching in troops ,If the birds are flying in groups

If the butterflies gather nectar in pair ,If the squirrels trill together in trouble

If the rivers of world meet at one ,Then why we only wish to walk lone

-human

When all left in I direst sides

Except them who directed

my side nothing to keep me adhere

if they're not here

O lord !I beg to thy in my prayers

To tie me in their every sphere

It's penchant to drive here unless

I see them here

- My apex lords

*

I'll leave and won't return for long ' I said but due to some reasons .I could not leave and realized how imperative it is to stay. These wrinkles on face tries to fill all in you to twinkle

-copies of thine (god) herein murky world of mine

Each day is bird-day -

to my birthday (as days are treacherous as lottery tickets)

The young me

After years the scoop

of vanilla Even its white couldn't hide the dark

Those bright birthday candles

Brought no light on the contrary shook

The delight of this very day icing with fright

This day comes

To continue the legacy

To add wretch to my sealed cracks

To add consistency

To my celebration celibacy

Without fairy lights but many gaslights

Stoking my searches for flights off such lights

On a dark night

After fed with rice

Left alone for the fights

when those tiny handsdid not know way to bite

I Felt – disturbed sleep of monthly hours

Now has lost wish to get up to see morning flowers

I cried to the knights

other hands were feeding

fire in dire

Consoled for the arrival of another

for me but she was the only one

lured to sleep like all what happen

was mere a rain shower

I shrieked

but couldn't be summoned up there

without summing up her part in my plot

so sent down back by lords to

mould me in a sword

that one night turned upright

my day as night

and night as day

I turned pragmatic

To all what was earlier was static

-rescued at the eleventh hour

*

A child whose

childhood is vacuumed of all love fumes

Rarely blooms in youth

Prunes all its budding stems

With Blunt sham

Jerry !be wary –umhmm

No longer they can carry

the burden make haste

They are awaiting

Thou to see on the land of gold or bold

Can't carry the same for long

There to expunge your worries

But can't spill berries

No longer can carry those expectations of having cranberries

On the knees and hands soon

will get merge into this land

Their eyes becoming heavy

so as to make you merry as

you are their cherry they are merry

but if you will carry berry you have to get marry

Odd thoughts make me scary

But see they're not dreary

Dreams are many but most is to see u merry

My jerry !

Just be wary this life is ferry of dairies of many

write your own without being scary jerry just be wary!

-To Our parents whom we subside with

books ,hooks, looks make their slog worth only in this very birth

I too get afraid

What's there in between my legs

A life giving mighty

Or deity of some tyrant

dissatisfied almighty

- Famine of feminine

Transitable burden

With time

We all forget those attractions

But forgetting without regret

Ease the burden on your chest

This burden become transitable

If you did your best and all what they

tried is to pull you out of your vest

your proximity was a apricity

you still chose to be cold

-Love a slippery idea

And a evasive action

*

The world robbed me of my beauty

And called it as my duty *-tilted responsibility*

*

Took me as oil

you wished floating on

And filtering out whenever u feel scorn

but I'm soil that devour all in its core

signalling end in all one galore

*

Heart in hands

Talking in bed

Politics in head

Stay out

-so open that need to close

*

If I'm not your dream

I neither wish entertaining

being your sad reality -not found in familiarities you see my similarities

How could I be

in my right sense with you

When your eyes were

only on my bank and sank

I hated my gender so much

That I cut to boy cut

And looked down on all of my kind

As meek and weak

But realized could only

copy As if first hand floppy

demolishing my inner emotions

In direction of this acting

cleared my false position for some toxins

M mannequin of man

Dressed ,undressed , wreathed , unpacked

without checking my breath

to satisfy others back

faxed with hands like a fact

looked agape as if shape

replaced on finding something reframed

it's better not to face

If the end is to efface that one face

Better not to turn whole to those alluring eyes

If the end is to part them with other eyes

*

That choke wasn't chop

So I decided to cope

That near was not dear

So I decided to by my own peer

That law wasn't legit

So I decided to leave it

-amending my vows

Paradox of window

If you'll peep inside from outdoors

In their windows Will make u homeless

if you'll look out from indoors

You'll settle inside

The view out will grapple

Your inner intellect ripples

Came round faces and cases

some were red from head

One was fed up to fled

While other was fresh like a green haze

The other one was looming with ‘blemishes after skirmishes

- with stains of love

while some abstain of love

Met after years

Asked if why

disappeared like rainbow after rain

Said didn't wish

being that acid rain on your window pane

That will erode your view with its filthy rain

Not even that retreating monsoon

Which with its wind will sweep away all your tinge

That will bring

catastrophe on its turn off

And will depart with no certainty of its advent

not worth of your salt and sight

not a goldsmith

who placed the lively me beside dead stones

but a wordsmith

who snap me out of that slag heap of nasty

creeps they pushed me on

-price for words

*

Uhh re still abide in my sights

And you say I'm bide for tall heights

I'm okay with your hollow spoke

But won't be able to skim through another Jhoke*

Leaving in lurch

In search for another heart

Wont bless with a Mirth

Retreat wherever thou I feel your dearth

*

Shadows Are Ambient

Eyes Are on Coefficient

-my super shield

*

Don't be a stuff of fiction

I'm already in so friction

-When felt a change in your diction

*

Not a scholar

But your seminal work

asked if on elevation yup ! I replied but out of your evaluation

-Not parched of love sips

groping a prodigy in me

*

Dear diary

I lost uhh !but not my words

-two inseparable couples in platonic relationship

*

You re the blessing Of one

I'm curse of many

-Teachings were mine

But lessons were yours"

*

When they've options they'll turn you down

As one of the pages they turn round

Underscoring the times you theft your rest

Tying kids on your chest

Working twenty seven as helpdesk

If I had ascended those height slone

How I let you descend me down-hill

In the times

Earmark for myself I bury myself

In times when I lose myself

I desperately want to find myself easily as if a book in shelf

-stop confusing yourself

*

Love with abject future is like a 'dive without height'

That touch tiled bottom unrehearsed

*

Teenage pass into nothingness

without knocking doors of aging

without any friendly vote

with bad memories of

dejections and unrest

high speed rocket of emotions

rollercoaster of imperfect impressions

Told you

I'm small plant

Anything in excess would

Fling me to death

I need to be nurtured

That you might get tire seeping in

While You poured me with venom water

To slash cut out my untimely

version Lead to your immersion

in the soil over logged with water

The one who leave in darkness is never

missed in dawn dear -asked me if I miss

Last page left

Thought of taking test

Found it was not best

Stalked this one with zest

Got into another fals nest

My spine pine for that divine

After seeking all designed kinds

World a conceptual space

Can see All as Booms well as dooms in all

In first leg

It may be like chewing bitter*neem* twig

But….

This feeling will reel under teeth soon like those rumoured myth

you'll relish the multi benefits

out of the pain inflicts

it'll become easier to swallow down

likewise some mellow music sound

-obstacles

“U berated my grace

Feels like brake

Buh’d won’t let it become my another shake

drain off disdain

say something sane

rectify your craze and see amaze

unable to heal ,Gather your zeal

Uhh ‘ll be on seal

-stop wailing till u avail

*

I love animals this much

That

I never made you scapegoat of love -is it sin ?

*

Fun that

Left buying bun

-you should undone

*

I was not part of any

I felt whole I was

-miscalculations

*

The best disinfectant

You can wash your brain with

is the touch of page -

perennial bribble of enlightenment

*

'If we are different

If things are different Then let's set apart

Let's Apart for the remaining

Let's leave for a while

Let's dive to the edge of different skies'

I was sitting with the right on left side

-as I wronged you for the right

*

Telling You about the day

Is my irresistible cuisine

-which I want to skip now

Tranquillity is treasure = Measure for pleasure

*

I've short temper

I woke up in the lust of pasta ; found it gobbled up The world seemed so cold and inconsiderate for the fully next fifteen minutes and mincing words did n leave me for the day I wonder how I suffered something that all was hamper without slight pamper .

*

Asked why I've no words in my dictionary

Told I stopped keeping the words that bear no meaning

*

Get up to morning

You'll get all answers from dilapidated sky

Which torn itself into Flakes in morning

And with night arrival turns black cover to heal

Those stars fading

To pop up your gateway In different ways

-After all ideological sink

I'm taking dip in realism

With my black moles

I fell foul on my

goals Which they called blackholes from evil zones

I crawled in whatever I got involved

I hobbled thy threshold

Tossed and tousled

Model of a hovel

From *brahmgiri* to find thee on my knees

From*c hitrakut* to find thy footmarks for tribute

From *rameshwaram* to find thy shadows in ocean zooms

Tones of triumphs and *harmoniums*

Carnatic rhythm and *mridang*

thumped in my monotonous

life lump and I rose to life with a jump

Want to complete thesis of life being a theist '

-cascade of joy

Doors shut the views

Windows are open

to all blues and clues

-My house is little

With big windows

Paarijaat and *kaartikmaas :*

For months

For a month

*Paarijaat*waits for *kaartik*

Every year

Both meet at night

In mild cold with bold heart

Like that tumultuous spring love

Which Spread aromatic flower shower

like some melodious flute in night mute

*at bhor** sorrow of infatuation

disturbs her saturation

she shred all of her beauty in devotion

while*kaartik*was leaving in motion

to a coarse green shrub without fashion

for another year for months

for a month

They called it “”"lovers tree Or tree of sadnesss

For meIt’s tree full of madness

*hindi word for dawn

A beautiful story

Hesimply had an attraction

That is why grabbed her all attention

While she had traction of joining fractioned

That's why completed the story

When the world sought no glory

-their ceilings were leaking But taught her to staunch the gulf fear of years

*

Oggy with its mumma

Heron with its heroic land on bull's hump

New grown bushes with its flaunting foliage

Temperature with its coolness All in glam

I'm with my usual silence and have Become used to this sound of no sound

.

-when a sound 'hushed' me to hell

*

scrounging for that Pristine

Be pearl a first Cocoon up in couth shell without any outer thrust

-Not a connoisseur can help you taste delicate real

*

the game you played justifed on petals

U met

But When!

when I was nibbling roses

That every petal to swallow the fact

'you love me not '

before my eyes sees

that hard on me as heavy metal

with preserving every petal with the fact

'u love me'

Nutritious to me as nettle

Night embarks on daykites

It turns dark Street starts joking

I hear aunties 'mocking'

And some guys smoking Checking my walkings

Dogs starts barking

Bats and some people starts hovering

Shadows shortening torch lights rolling respected knuckle

Nohh !sorry respected uncle

I feel sorry for your hawking eyes

Selling disgrace and lies Hiding the files

Of stalking me at night

Zooming out wide staggering for invite

I started missing gods

While wishing for short row for my home

Without stretched brows of foes on ways afraid of their

gruesome laws which in turn will find flaws

resting me in funeral journal

with the first ray of shine

the one surrender in sleep

is truly out of lively world

who grabbed their bed sheets

hardly covering them as alive corpse

*

The myriad of bird chirrup is the best music one can suggest to me

-without ads

*

Ina fix whether flee or to glee

Dared to drink But didn't dispatched

That 'oison even did not wish

Me to become only frame 'Icon.

You're that recurring thought Like my stubborn curl

I stretch to straighten But get back to its real place

*

What my writings are doing –

paving green way for those

who don't have companions on road to walk with

*

Politics and poetry

We keep words they erase

We keep mugs they thugs

We treat with poems they with

*

I won't ask you for big mansions the utmost is to mention me in your ventures

- debunking your thoughts

*

Asked for a promise

That you'll not be frown if I drown without inform

all what which seem so sound if turns to pyre in one round

*

Love a mist or feast

Fragile me in fix

But aware of gist

After eye mist

All get fix

mind forebodings

18 aug

I missed the once in blue moon moon -moon the super moon of this year

The thing about stars is that

They ignite in a fleet

On all bleak and brittle night sheets

Without caring if sky

is polluted or rain diluted

Unlike moon that hides

it's eminence Shine brightly and lightly

beams only when it's gleam; when it'full

And pays only for a tinker like tenants

Despite the onus we boast as bonus

Extended to it as honour

Spending all night looking

umpteenth time as if the last falling milk teeth

I Was a wizard

Slammed by wicked

Glibly got under hammer

Scrounged for stalwart

Menace that was Duped of love

Shred in one go

Fancied initially for pewter

Turn me to a poor debtor

Streak of eerie beckoned

Eloped after it Subsided with humor

Stucked my head out

Dragged on a thunder

Dinghies of memories

Retreating to stranded sights

Accused of derogatory ships

Starboard side sealed ,Ship perplexed for another night

Pox erupted

And he broke out of my skin

disfiguring my every part left me figuring

How entered the skin like essential zinc

And drained out in wink

wanted to slap this crack

But instead I patted my back

And continued my wreck

Considering myself as seller of love

Which you thought of "confiscating" at a bargained price

or that Ayurveda panacea you can never find

-damp squib

Too late to realise on wheel chair now with pairs of wheel Then why I cared for that third wheel

*

I'm *Kesar*

I get dissolve into warm locals

and soothing vocals

leaving my cherished

tinge on their focals

*

I explored *Benaras* through his voice

Which left in my invoice

And my mind questioned why ?

I became debtor with choice

I replied 'I rejoice only this noise

You made me

feel like an outdated language

In world of slangs

An unapprehensible voluminous tittle

thumbed at edges in dusty compound

It's been long

we should meet it's been long

we should see it's been long

we should talk communication is key

i worry is it necessary to beat ear drums or tear eyes for fun

if meeting you means forgetting myself

let's never meet ,let's this distance seed some need

Fine !why fine !

Where contentment will be high

And skies will kisses the flies. I'll meet you there fine !

And it's no longer bias and byees .I'll be there with u fine

no longer shy but with fiiii I'll meet u there fine

I'm happier here some way

'llcwtch you some other day while dine

Devoid of counterbalance

Will make u gloom soon

But I'm dying to shine

'll call u some other day mine

Fine !

With all this I terminate here to embark higher .I apologise for the mistakes , errors in spelling and my sadist words .lots of respect and affection for the one who read it and made my work felt worth . my ending note should be door opening to many .

"Thou mere join two plain plank of hands humanity will be
bridged in this mere attempt"

about author
shirvelled up in spring
tropical in winter
insensitive cold in summer

www.ingramcontent.com/pod-product-compliance
Lightning Source LLC
LaVergne TN
LVHW090131160826
845673LV00017B/2081

9798896106180